World at Risk

WATER

Geoff Barker

A+

Smart Apple Media

Smart Apple Media
P.O. Box 3263
Mankato, MN 56002

Printed in the United States of America

Library of Congress Cataloging-in-Publication Data

Barker, Geoff.
  Water / by Geoff Barker.
     p. cm. -- (World at risk)
  Includes index.
  ISBN 978-1-59920-379-9 (hardcover)
  1. Water--Juvenile literature. 2. Water conservation--Juvenile literature. I. Title.
  GB662.3.B39 2010
  553.7--dc22

                              2009006356

Created by Q2AMedia
Editor: Anand Mani/Katie Dicker
Art Director: Rahul Dhiman
Designer: Harleen Mehta
Picture Researchers: Anju Pathak, Shreya Sharma
Line Artist: Sibi N. Devasia
Colouring Artist: Aadil Ahmad
Technical Artists: Abhideep Jha, Bibin Jose, Manoj Joshi

All words in **bold** can be found in the glossary on pages 42–43.

Web site information is correct at time of going to press. However, the publishers cannot
accept liability for any information or links found on third-party web sites.

Picture credits
t=top b=bottom c=center l=left r=right

Cover Images: Shutterstock: bg, Inset: Collin stitt/ Shutterstock: cl, shutterstock: c, shutterstock: cr.

Insides: Mashe/ Shutterstock: 3, NASA: 8, Wolfgang Amri/ Shutterstock: 9, Eduardo Rivero/ Shutterstock: 11, Michael Fuery/ Shutterstock:
13, David Turnley/ Corbis: 14, Ewen/ Dreamstime: 17, Jan kranendonk/ Shutterstock: 18, Associated Press: 19, Natalie Fobes/ Getty Images:
21, Custom Cards/ iStockphoto: 22, Kevin Schafer/ Alamy: 23, Pozzo Diborgo Thomas/ Shutterstock: 24-25, Nello Giambi/ Getty Images: 26,
Dado Galdieri/ Associated Press: 28, Soopy Sue/ iStockphoto: 29, Tad Denson/ Shutterstock: 30, Doctor Kan/ iStockphoto: 31, Itsuo Inouye/
Associated Press: 32, Gerd Ludwig/ Corbis: 33, imagebroker / Alamy: 35, Sasha Radosavljevich/ Shutterstock: 36, Attar Maher/ Corbis Sygma:
37, Enlightened Images/ Photolibrary: 38, FloridaStock/ Shutterstock: 39,

Q2AMedia Art Bank: 10, 12, 16, 20, 27, 34, 41.

9 8 7 6 5 4 3 2 1

CONTENTS

1

WATER FOR LIFE

Why do so many of us take water for granted? Tasteless, odorless, and transparent, water seems to be all around. But life would not exist on our "blue planet" without water.

Life on Earth

Water covers nearly three-quarters of the Earth's surface. This liquid water is essential for life. It enabled the first organisms to form on Earth billions of years ago, and it has sustained animal and plant life ever since. In fact, when scientists look for signs of life on other planets, they initially look for past or present evidence of water.

There is so much water on Earth that it appears like a blue planet when seen from space.

Water for Plants and Animals

Water makes the Earth different from other planets —every living thing on Earth depends on water to survive. Like humans, animals eat and drink to maintain a balance of water in their bodies. This keeps their cells functioning properly. Plants use their roots to take in water from the soil. This water is full of minerals and nutrients that help their cells to grow and repair themselves. Plants pass water vapor out through their leaves. At night, they lose very little water through their leaves, but on hot days, they return a lot of water to the atmosphere.

Water in the Human Body

About 70 percent of the human body is water, and it carries out many vital functions. A great **solvent**, water can **dissolve** chemicals such as salts and enable them to move around the body with ease. Water also supports vital processes and systems.

It transports blood and food around the body and helps to remove waste products quickly and efficiently. The body also needs water to maintain a steady temperature and to help joints move.

Feeling Thirsty?

Water is crucial for survival. We can go for a month without food, but we will die after three to five days without any water. Our body loses water when we breathe out, sweat, and urinate. We can replace this water from some of the food we eat, but we also need to drink plenty of water each day to keep our bodies functioning at their best. We feel thirsty or dehydrated when the quantity of water we have consumed is less than the quantity of water our body has lost. When we are dehydrated, salt levels in the blood rise and nerve cells in our brain trigger the desire to drink.

A huge variety of plants and animals survive in the various water habitats found on Earth, such as rivers, ponds, oceans, and lakes.

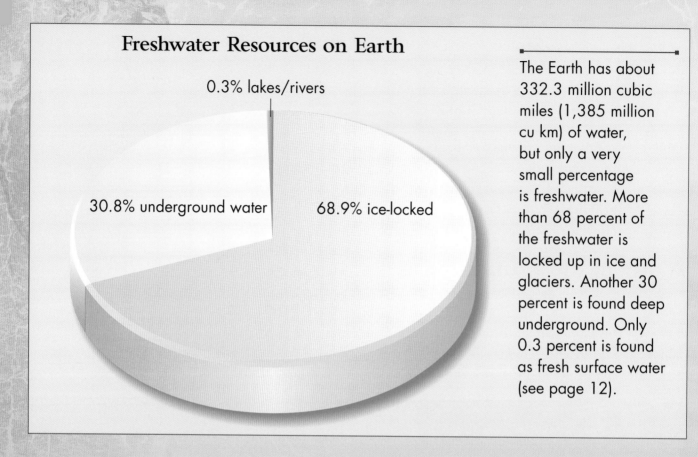

Freshwater Resources on Earth

0.3% lakes/rivers

30.8% underground water

68.9% ice-locked

The Earth has about 332.3 million cubic miles (1,385 million cu km) of water, but only a very small percentage is freshwater. More than 68 percent of the freshwater is locked up in ice and glaciers. Another 30 percent is found deep underground. Only 0.3 percent is found as fresh surface water (see page 12).

Unique Substance

Water is a simple chemical compound made from two **atoms** of hydrogen and one atom of oxygen. Scientists represent it with the symbol H_2O. The hydrogen atoms in water are constantly moving from one **molecule** to another. This gives water its liquid quality. The molecules in a glass of water, for example, are constantly forming and reforming.

Solid, Liquid, and Gas

Another characteristic of water is that it can exist on Earth in three different forms, or states of matter—as a solid, a liquid, or a gas. It can easily switch between the different states, depending on the temperature. When water is heated, it changes to a gas, known as water vapor. When the temperature is lowered, liquid water freezes and becomes ice. Solid ice takes up more space than liquid water because the atoms are arranged in a crystal-like structure. This also makes ice less dense than water, which explains why ice floats.

Water Cycle

The ability of water to change from one form to another can be seen in what is known as the water cycle. Water moves continuously on Earth, changing and transforming all around us. The sun heats the water in the oceans, rivers, and lakes, for example, causing the water to change state and become water vapor. This is known as **evaporation**. In the atmosphere, the water vapor cools and condenses to form clouds. This cooled water vapor falls to the ground as rain, sleet, hail, or snow in a process called **precipitation**. The water collects in streams and rivers and pours into lakes or flows straight back to the seas and oceans to begin the cycle again.

Freshwater

About 97 percent of the water on Earth is contained in seas and oceans and is too salty for us to drink. Of all the freshwater on Earth, only about 0.3 percent—1 million cubic miles (4 million cu km)—is contained in rivers and lakes. The rest is more difficult to access (see page 10). Yet rivers and lakes are where most of the water we use in our everyday lives comes from.

Waste and Pollution

Since there is so little usable water on Earth, the way we treat this water has serious consequences for all life on the planet. **Pollution** and waste are the two biggest threats that our freshwater resources face. Pollution reduces the amount of clean water that is available to us. If we waste water or use it carelessly, we are not making the best use of the water that we have.

Most of the Earth's freshwater is locked up in ice caps and glaciers.

PLANET WATCH

» Lake Chad in Africa has shrunk 90 percent in size in a period of 40 years. This is partly due to a rise in the Earth's temperature.

» In 1986, a nuclear accident in Chernobyl, Ukraine, **contaminated** the water sources in the region. As a result, water found near the site is no longer used for drinking.

2

CLEAN WATER AND WASTEWATER

We are constantly using more and more water. During the last century, the world population tripled and the world consumption of water multiplied six times.

Freshwater Underground

About 30 percent of the freshwater on Earth is found deep underground. Rainwater falls and collects beneath the ground, where it is held in **porous** rocks called **aquifers**. Many countries with a very hot and dry **climate** depend on aquifers. In Egypt, for example, the only source of freshwater for the country's western district—an area of about 435,000 square miles (700,000 sq km)—is the Nubian Sandstone Aquifer. Situated under Egypt,

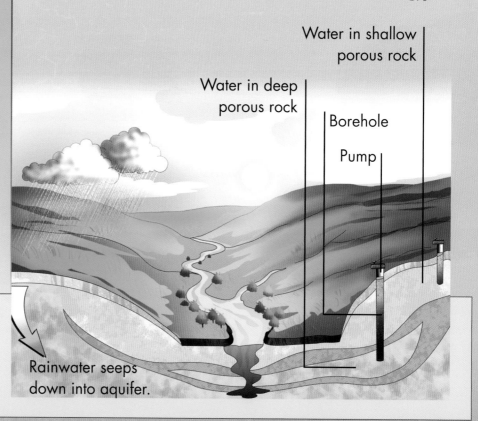

Water in shallow porous rock

Water in deep porous rock

Borehole

Pump

Rainwater seeps down into aquifer.

Water trapped in porous rock deep underground is often brought up to the surface using boreholes.

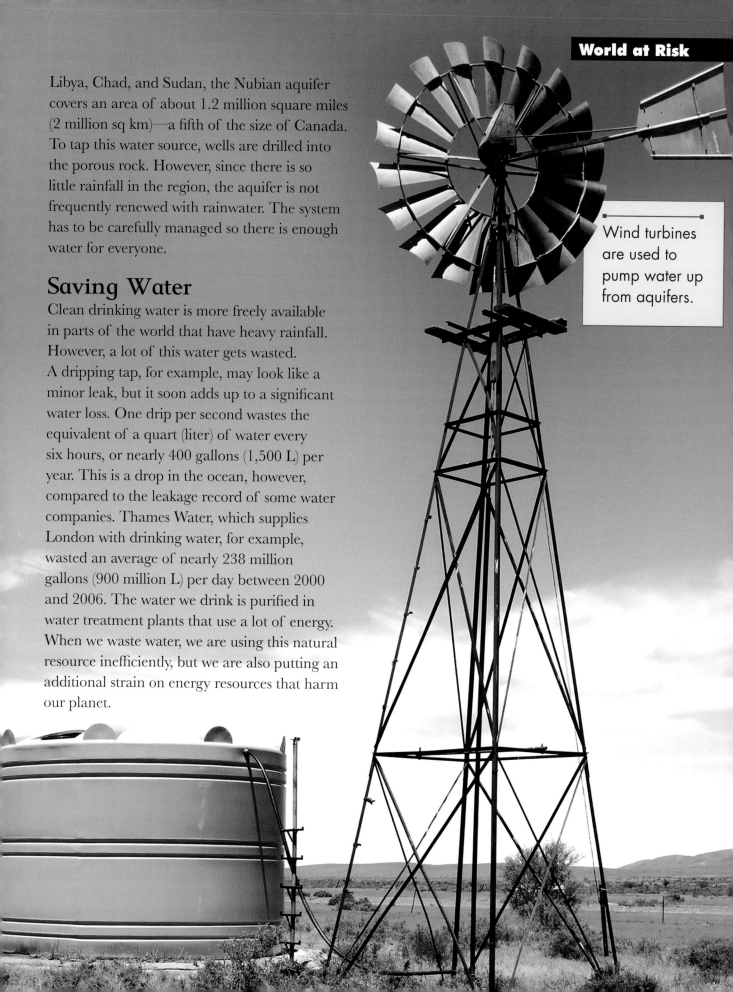

Libya, Chad, and Sudan, the Nubian aquifer covers an area of about 1.2 million square miles (2 million sq km)—a fifth of the size of Canada. To tap this water source, wells are drilled into the porous rock. However, since there is so little rainfall in the region, the aquifer is not frequently renewed with rainwater. The system has to be carefully managed so there is enough water for everyone.

Saving Water

Clean drinking water is more freely available in parts of the world that have heavy rainfall. However, a lot of this water gets wasted. A dripping tap, for example, may look like a minor leak, but it soon adds up to a significant water loss. One drip per second wastes the equivalent of a quart (liter) of water every six hours, or nearly 400 gallons (1,500 L) per year. This is a drop in the ocean, however, compared to the leakage record of some water companies. Thames Water, which supplies London with drinking water, for example, wasted an average of nearly 238 million gallons (900 million L) per day between 2000 and 2006. The water we drink is purified in water treatment plants that use a lot of energy. When we waste water, we are using this natural resource inefficiently, but we are also putting an additional strain on energy resources that harm our planet.

Wind turbines are used to pump water up from aquifers.

Access to Clean Water

In more economically developed countries (**MEDCs**), people have greater access to clean, safe water. But even in these countries, the water comes from limited underground aquifers, lakes, and rivers. Water from these sources has to go through a process of **purification** before it is safe to drink.

Journey to the Taps

Water needs to be cleaned and piped to our homes before we can use it. Rainwater from **reservoirs** is usually drained through sand and gravel to filter out any dirt and dust. Harmful, microscopic bacteria found in dirty water are eliminated by adding chemicals, such as chlorine. Storage tanks keep large supplies of this filtered, purified water before it is pumped through large underground pipes called mains. Water flows through the mains to smaller pipes as they run closer to homes, schools, and factories. The pipes get smaller still until they reach the many taps that we turn on whenever we want to drink, cook, wash, or clean.

No Bathtub, No Toilet

Not everyone has access to a toilet, sink, or bathtub, however. Around 4.6 billion people (from a world population of 6.7 billion) live in less economically developed countries (**LEDCs**). For many people in parts of Africa and Asia, for example, water is a rare resource valued as a matter of life and death. Nearly half the people in the world live in **drought** conditions and do not have a clean place to wash themselves or go to the bathroom. Some have to walk for several hours a day to get to a water pump or stream, and then they carry the water back for their families in large, heavy containers.

In many parts of the world, water is so scarce that people have to travel great distances to get clean, safe water.

Where Water Is Scarce

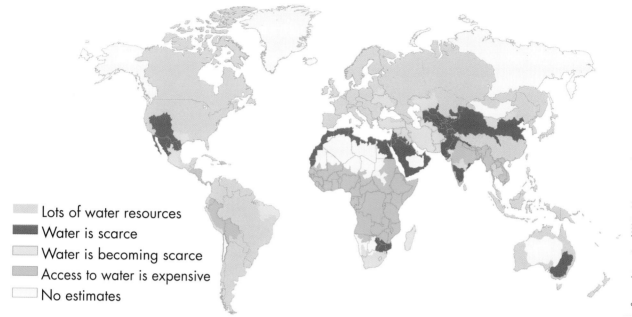

Lots of water resources
Water is scarce
Water is becoming scarce
Access to water is expensive
No estimates

Source: International Water Management Institute

Freshwater resources are divided very unevenly across the world. Access to water depends on location, but financial resources play a part, too.

Dirty Water

Even deadlier than drought is disease caused by dirty water. One in five people around the world have no access to clean, safe drinking water. Dirty water is the world's single greatest killer—around 5,000 children die from drinking dirty water every day. **Diarrhea**, caused by drinking or having contact with dirty, infected water, causes children to become dehydrated and to lose essential salts and nutrients from their bodies. Diarrhea alone kills as many as 1.8 million young children every year.

Flood Water

Dirty water can affect MEDCs, too. Sometimes floods and storms disrupt the pumps and pipes that provide our water, and clean supplies become contaminated. In 2005, for example, the floods in New Orleans after Hurricane Katrina caused supplies of drinking water to mix with flood water and sewage. Luckily, scientists have developed water purification techniques to overcome these situations. In the case of Hurricane Katrina, purification destroyed more than 99 percent of harmful bacteria found in the water supplies. The water was still undrinkable, but it could be safely used for washing and cleaning.

PLANET WATCH

» It is thought that 2.6 billion people in the world do not have proper **sanitation** facilities.

» In 2006, the United Nations Development Program reported that 1.1 billion people around the world do not have access to safe drinking water.

» The number of households connected to sewers in major cities varies greatly across the globe. In North America, the figure is 96 percent, in Asia 45 percent, and in Africa, only 18 percent.

Recycling Wastewater

Every day we produce hundreds of gallons of wastewater. This water can be treated and reintroduced into the water cycle. Wastewater from the sink, bathtub, or toilet goes to a sewage treatment plant. The first step is to filter out large solids such as feces. Other solids are left to settle, and the wastewater is carefully filtered again before standing in special beds where **friendly bacteria** kill and remove harmful **microbes**. The water is then disinfected with **ultraviolet (UV) light** or chlorine. The purified water has to meet health and safety standards before it is allowed to flow back into rivers or lakes, where it is reintroduced into the water supply. Meanwhile, the leftover **sludge** from the sewage treatment is a useful resource. The methane gas it produces is burned to generate electricity. The sludge can also be used by farmers on the land as **fertilizer**.

Most MEDCs have sewage treatment processes in place. This ensures that all wastewater is cleaned up before it is introduced back into the environment.

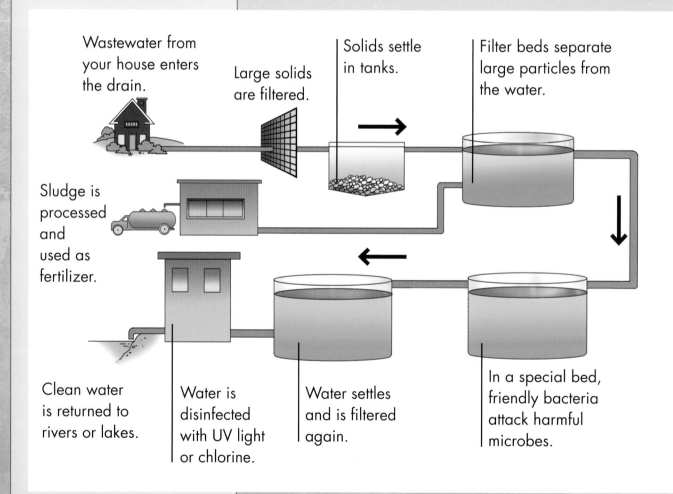

Wastewater from your house enters the drain.

Large solids are filtered.

Solids settle in tanks.

Filter beds separate large particles from the water.

Sludge is processed and used as fertilizer.

In a special bed, friendly bacteria attack harmful microbes.

Clean water is returned to rivers or lakes.

Water is disinfected with UV light or chlorine.

Water settles and is filtered again.

In these large filter beds in a sewage treatment plant, heavy sediment falls to the bottom while the water is filtered out.

Wastewater in Australia

Although wastewater is recycled in many countries, such as the United States and the United Kingdom, the process is less popular in other parts of the world. In Australia, water was not recycled for many years. It was only in 2007, when drought conditions became so bad, that a policy was put in place. The Australian state of Queensland is currently setting up water treatment plants to provide drinking water from recycled wastewater. Due to drought conditions in recent years, the Queensland Water Commission predicts that Queensland's reservoirs could be dry by 2009. Although many Australians dislike the idea of drinking recycled water, weather conditions could force all Australian states to drink purified wastewater in the near future.

New Recycling Ideas

Scientists are finding other ways to recycle the water that we use. Huge amounts of water are wasted in the manufacture of beers and wines, for example. This water contains sugar, starch, and alcohol, but scientists at the University of Queensland have found a way of removing these wastes and recycling the water. Sugar-consuming bacteria are used to clean the water and can also make energy in the process. In Australia's largest brewery in Brisbane, sugar-eating bacteria are expected to generate enough electricity to power a large household for 24 hours by using a thousandth of the wastewater the brewery generates every day. The recycled, purified water at the end of the process is also drinkable, which could help to solve Queensland's water problems.

Planet Watch

» Australia's worst ever drought began in 2002 and continued through 2008. These conditions severely affected the production of water-irrigated crops.

» Australia used to produce 1.8 million tons (1.6 million t) of rice a year. This dropped to 117,000 tons (106,000 t) in 2006–7. Due to the continuing drought, there may be no rice harvest at all in future years.

3

WATER POLLUTION

When we pollute water, we make it dirty or poisonous. This threatens our water supplies and has a serious effect on plants and animals, too.

Waterside Communities

Towns and cities all over the world have grown up close to rivers and lakes. These natural features encouraged people to settle because they provided a ready supply of water for drinking, cooking, cleaning, and growing crops. Flowing water was also a useful form of transportation and a quick way to get rid of unwanted garbage. Today, some factories around the world continue to pump poisonous waste products and chemicals into nearby seas and rivers.

Water can dissolve many materials, but some waste products cause long-term pollution problems. Chemicals, plastics, and metals, for example, are poisonous to many living things and do not **decompose** easily. These materials can threaten our freshwater resources, and the pollution has a serious effect on the plants and animals that depend on the water for their survival.

Earth Data

- The seas and oceans are a primary source of food for more than 3.5 billion people around the world. This number could double to 7 billion within 20 years.

- In 90 percent of cities in LEDCs, sewage is pumped straight into rivers, lakes, and seas without treating it.

- More than half the world's coral reefs are endangered because of chemicals and waste dumped at sea.

- Between 1932 and 1968, the Chisso chemical factory in Japan dumped an estimated 30 tons (27 t) of mercury compounds into the sea at Minamata Bay (see page 19).

The white foam on the surface of this water indicates that harmful chemical wastes have caused pollution.

Poisoning Wildlife

Garbage—including waste food, dead animals, and sewage—can pollute water supplies and poison wildlife. Some towns and cities do not clean sewage sufficiently before returning the wastewater to rivers and streams. Others pour raw sewage straight into the sea. Sewage can poison wildlife in the water, and harmful bacteria can cause disease and infection. Sewage also uses oxygen when it decomposes. This means there is less oxygen in the water for living creatures. Industries can help to reduce water pollution by removing harmful substances from wastewater before it is returned to rivers, streams, and oceans.

Poisoning People

In 1956, an unknown disease broke out in Minamata, a city on the coast of the Japanese island of Kyushu. The disease, which became known as Minamata disease, affected the **central nervous system**, causing a lack of coordination and, in extreme cases, coma and death. The victims often lived by the coast and mainly ate fish and shellfish. Researchers discovered that Minamata disease was, in fact, severe mercury poisoning caused by eating contaminated seafood. A chemical factory nearby had been dumping wastewater with low concentrations of methyl mercury into Minamata Bay for more than 30 years. Nearly 2,000 people died as a result of the disease. The pollutants passed up the marine **food chain** as large marine animals ate smaller creatures. This caused the mercury to increase in concentration until it reached **toxic** levels. When humans, at the top of the food chain, ate fish and shellfish, they were at great risk of poisoning.

By March 2001, more than 2,000 victims of Minamata disease had been officially recognized. Of these, 1,784 had died of the disease.

Oil Spills

In August 2006, the oil tanker *Solar I* sank in deep water off the Philippines. It was the country's worst oil spill. About 53,000 gallons (200,000 L) of oil leaked into the ocean, covering nearly 200 miles (320 km) of coastline and destroying marine wildlife and a huge area of coral reef. Before long, a further 476,000 gallons (1.8 million L) of fuel stored in the sunken vessel escaped to inflict even more damage on the marine environment of the Philippines.

When this type of **ecological** crisis happens, seabirds, marine mammals, and fish are all affected. Most of the oil floats and forms huge **slicks** on the water's surface. Birds and mammals swallow toxic oil as they try to clean themselves. Fish absorb the black tarlike oil through their gills and from direct contact. When people try to clean up the disaster, it is often too late for wildlife, and many seabirds have too much oil on their feathers to be cleaned.

Unlike the *Solar I* oil tanker, new oil tankers have to be built with a double hull. This means that even if the outer hull is pierced by rocks, the inner hull—containing oil—remains intact.

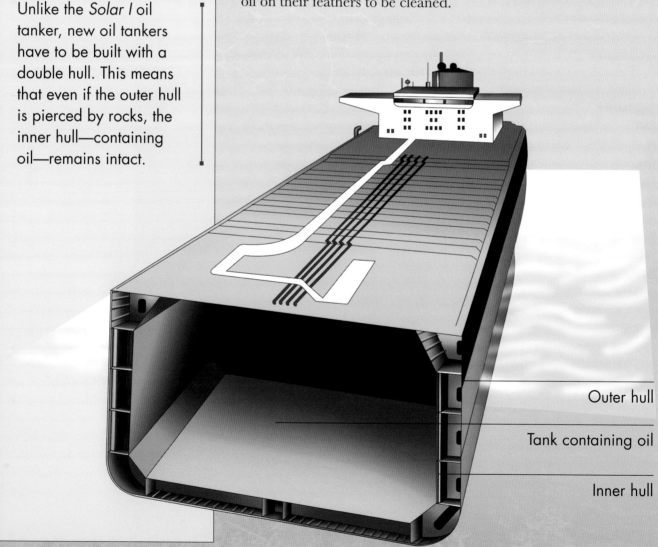

Outer hull

Tank containing oil

Inner hull

After a cleanup with soapy detergents, this bird may live. Most will not survive.

Down the Drain

Oil tanker accidents such as the *Solar I* in the Philippines always grab the headlines. But these accidents account for a very small amount of marine pollution. The U.S. National Science Foundation, for example, found that only 2 percent of oil pollution actually comes from oil tanker accidents. Although it is against the law, many oil tankers clean out their tanks at sea to save time in port. What is even more surprising is that 50 percent of marine oil pollution comes from rivers that have drained into the sea. Old engine oil dumped down the drain or buried in the soil, for example, eventually ends up in the sea. Other sources of marine pollution include sewage, industrial and radioactive waste, and poisonous leakage from landfills.

Overuse of Detergents

Detergents are often used to disperse oil slicks at sea, but they are also familiar in our homes and are widely used in industry. If detergents are used in large enough quantities, they can produce toxic effects in all types of **aquatic** life. Detergents destroy the thin film that a fish has to protect itself from parasites and bacteria. Most fish die when concentrations of detergent rise to around 15 parts per million (ppm) of water. But concentrations as low as 5 ppm can kill fish eggs.

Detergents also allow harmful pesticides and chemicals to mix into the water. As a result, fish and other aquatic life absorb them. A detergent concentration of only 2 ppm can cause fish to absorb twice the amount of chemicals that they would normally take in.

PLANET WATCH

» When the oil tanker *Exxon Valdez* ran aground off the coast of Alaska in 1989, half a million seabirds and hundreds of wild animals were killed by the oil spill.

» In 1978, The *Amoco Cadiz* lost more than 254,000 tons (230,000 t) of oil off the coast of France.

21

Hazardous chemicals found in fertilizers and pesticides often find their way into the water cycle.

Farming

Farming makes huge demands on our water resources—as much as 70 percent of all water used worldwide is for agriculture. The main use is for **irrigation**—the crops that humans and livestock eat need regular supplies of water. Farming also contributes to water pollution. Many farmers spray their crops with fertilizers and pesticides. The fertilizers help plants to grow even bigger, and the pesticides kill pests that damage them. Over time, these chemicals can build up in the soil to harmful levels, threatening water sources and wildlife nearby.

Some chemicals seep down into underground water sources or run into rivers, lakes, and seas.

They contaminate the water and are a threat to aquatic creatures. Sometimes, the chemicals cause tiny water plants, called algae, to grow more rapidly in lakes and rivers. If this algae spreads quickly over the water's surface, it can cut off light and oxygen supplies—vital sources of energy that larger plants and fish depend on. As these algae multiply, they form huge blankets, called algal blooms, over the surface of the water. And when these algae die, the problems get worse. Bacteria that feed on the dead algae increase in number. They use dissolved oxygen in the water to decompose the algae. This means that essential oxygen levels in the water decline even further, putting aquatic plants and animals at an even greater risk.

Red Tides

When algae numbers increase dramatically in this way, they can discolor water, making it red, brown, yellow, or green. Despite the different colors, these algal blooms are commonly known as "red tides." Human activities, such as farming, contribute significantly to many algal blooms, but others seem to occur naturally. Some blooms produce toxins that have a serious effect on wildlife. We call them harmful algal blooms (HABs). When toxins are consumed by marine creatures, they become even more concentrated as they move up the food chain (see page 19). Humans can be poisoned if they eat affected fish or shellfish.

Red tides have occurred nearly every year in late summer and early autumn in the Gulf of Mexico for at least 50 years. Although there are more than 40 species of HABs in the Gulf of Mexico, the most common species of algae found there is the Florida red tide organism (*Karenia brevis*). The toxins that it produces can kill fish, birds, and other marine animals. These can cause health problems for humans. Symptoms of shellfish poisoning include diarrhea, dizziness, and temporary numbness of the mouth. Florida monitors the **tides** in this region carefully and now bans the harvesting of shellfish during high concentrations of algal blooms.

Algal blooms are often known as red tides. They can be very toxic to marine life.

PLANET WATCH

» Some foods are produced using more water than others. It takes more than 2,000 gallons (7,569 L) to produce 1 pound (.45 kg) of beef, but 1 pound (.45 kg) of potatoes takes 66 gallons (250 L).

» Around 70 percent of all crops grown depend entirely on irrigation water. Only a third of this water is actually absorbed by the plants, however. The remainder is lost.

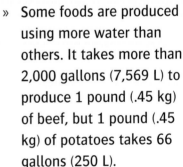

Acid Rain

Sometimes, rainwater becomes polluted and unsafe to drink. When rainwater mixes with polluting chemicals in the air, it forms acid rain. This rain falls into streams, rivers, and lakes, polluting the water.

Acid rain is caused when water vapor mixes with polluting gases such as sulfur dioxide and nitrogen oxides. These gases are produced by factories and power plants that burn fossil fuels, and cars and trucks that belch out gasoline and diesel fumes. The polluting gases mix with water to form dilute sulfuric acid and nitric acid. Acid rain is usually most severe around large industrial or urban areas, but it can also be carried by the wind.

Unpolluted rain is slightly acidic—with a **pH value** of five or six—because it mixes with naturally occurring oxides in the air. However, polluted rain can have a pH value of two or three, making it strong enough to damage trees, kill fish, and erode stone structures.

This unique mineral forest is found in the Morondava region of Madagascar. These rock shapes can be caused by water erosion and acid rain carried by the wind.

Damage to Trees

Acid rain damages trees and other plants by washing away vital nutrients and minerals in the soil around their roots. Acid rain can also wear away the protective waxy coating on the leaves, reducing their ability to **photosynthesize**. Trees weakened by acid rain are less able to fight disease and insect attacks.

Damage to Animals

Acid rain runs off the land into rivers and lakes. Freshwater shrimp and snails are two species that are badly affected by acid rain. When one species disappears, it upsets the delicate balance of the **food web**, and other species feeding on it can start to disappear, too. Whole **ecosystems** can be affected in this way. Acid rain also washes aluminum compounds out of the soil, and these compounds are highly toxic to aquatic creatures.

Acid Rain Solutions

Lakes can recover from the effects of acid rain if the acidity of the water is reduced or **neutralized**. An **alkaline** substance called powdered lime (calcium hydroxide) can be added to the acidic water to reduce the acidity. However, this process, called "liming," is expensive and does not tackle the root cause of the problem.

Ways to reduce acid rain include using fewer fossil fuels and burning fossil fuels more efficiently, so they produce less pollution. Governments are beginning to cut pollution in their countries. Since 1975, for example, U.S. car manufacturers have used catalytic converters to control dangerous chemicals in exhaust fumes. According to the U.S. Environmental Protection Agency, current vehicles emit up to 98 percent less of these chemicals than vehicles sold in the early 1970s.

PLANET WATCH

» In recent years, Sweden has been exposed to high levels of acid rain caused by pollution carried by the winds from other parts of the world. More than 18,000 Swedish lakes have become so acidic that all the fish have died.

» A huge metal mining company in Norilsk, Siberia, is thought to be the world's largest producer of acid rain. It is thought that 1 percent of the planet's sulfur dioxide emissions come from this city alone.

4

GLOBAL WARMING

The Earth's temperature is gradually rising. The heat is having an effect on water sources, too. Most scientists agree that we need to act against the causes of global warming.

Earth Data

- Average temperatures in Europe have risen by 1.37°F (0.76°C) in the past 100 years. Temperatures are likely to rise by a further 3.6 to 10.8°F (2 to 6°C) this century if **carbon emissions** continue to build up.

- The European Union has set a target to limit the rise in average global temperatures by no more than 3.6°F (2°C). However, this temperature rise is likely to be exceeded by 2040 to 2070.

- Natural gas produces less carbon dioxide than other fossil fuels. Emissions from a natural gas power plants are about five percent carbon dioxide. Emissions from a coal power plant can be three times as high.

Greenhouse Effect

Every day we use gasoline or diesel fuel to run our cars. We also burn fossil fuels in power plants to make electricity and to heat our homes. When these fuels are burned, they release carbon dioxide and methane, which rise to form an invisible blanket around the Earth. These gases let the heat of the sun through, but stop some of this heat escaping back to space. We call this "the greenhouse effect" because the gases absorb heat (just as the air in a greenhouse gets hot in the sunshine). Scientists believe that an increase in these **greenhouse gases** is gradually making our planet warmer. We call this process **global warming**.

Car exhaust fumes pollute our environment and add to the effect of global warming.

Melting Sea Ice

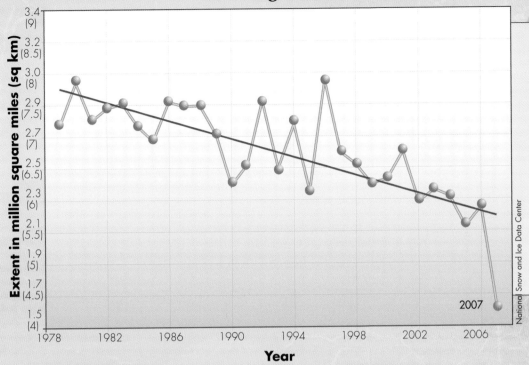

This graph shows the amount of ice in the sea in September each year from 1979 to 2007. Until recently, the ice has declined by about 10 percent every 10 years.

National Snow and Ice Data Center

Meltdown

Global warming is causing the Earth's ice to melt at an alarming rate. Mountain and polar ice caps and **glaciers** are disappearing fast. Scientists at the National Snow and Ice Data Center (NSIDC) in Colorado monitor and study Arctic sea ice, which is seen as a key indicator of climate change. They measure exactly how much sea ice melts during the Arctic summer. Ten years ago, scientists were predicting that within 100 years we would have an ice-free Arctic Ocean in summer. But over the years, this prediction has been brought forward. In 2007, researchers saw a record-breaking ice melt. As NSIDC senior scientist Mark Serreze explains, "The sea ice cover is in a downward spiral and may have passed the point of no return . . . We may well see an ice-free Arctic Ocean in summer within our lifetimes."

Although the summer melting of Arctic sea ice alone will not have a major impact on sea levels around the world, melting glaciers on land—such as the Greenland ice sheet and Antarctic ice shelf—will together have a huge impact.

Rising Sea Levels

Global warming is heating the seas and oceans. When water heats up, it expands, and, as a result, sea levels are rising. This is putting some countries at great risk. Much of Bangladesh, for example, is a flat **delta**, liable to flooding. Increased rainfall, **cyclones**, and snow melt from the Himalayas all contribute to the flooding in Bangladesh. But if tides are high, too, floodwater no longer drains into the ocean, and flooding can become disastrous. In the South Asian floods of 2007, 7.5 million Bangladeshis had to flee their homes, and about 400 people died.

Will Europe Freeze Over?

The **Gulf Stream** in the North Atlantic is an ocean current that keeps western Europe warm. If climate change disrupts the Gulf Stream, the United Kingdom and France could become as cold as Canada. The average temperature in Paris, France, is 51.8°F (11°C), while Quebec, Canada (at a similar **latitude**), has an average temperature of just 39.2°F (4°C).

Melting Glaciers

With 97 percent of the planet's water being salty sea water, we have just 3 percent freshwater at our disposal. About 69 percent of this freshwater is locked up in glaciers and in the ice caps of the polar regions. Changes in the climate, caused by global warming, are causing glaciers to melt at an alarming rate.

In the Lake Titicaca river basin in South America, the glaciers of Peru and Bolivia are experiencing significant losses. Between 1960 and 2003, for example, the Chacaltaya glacier lost 97 percent of its mass, and it is expected to disappear completely by 2010. Glaciers are the chief water source for many towns and cities near the Andes mountain range. Glaciers are used for the irrigation systems in the Altiplano (Spanish for "high plain") and in the dry desert area along the Pacific coast of Peru. The receding glaciers could mean drought for thousands of Peruvian and Bolivian people.

This scientist is measuring the thickness of the Chacaltaya glacier in Bolivia. Global warming is causing the glacier to melt away.

The majestic ice cap of Mount Kilimanjaro in Africa could disappear by 2020.

Ice Hunters

In the icier reaches of northern Canada, Inuit populations have lived across an area of about 772,200 square miles (2 million sq km) for the past 5,000 years. But today their lifestyles are in a process of change. Traditional skills of reading the ice as they hunt for food have had to be supplemented with the latest satellite navigation technology. During the spring melt, the Inuit can no longer safely travel across the **ice floes** without this up-to-date information. As a member of the Inuit Circumpolar Conference, an international organization representing the Inuit, said, "the Earth is literally changing beneath our feet."

Polar Bears under Threat

The effects of global warming are more extreme at the Earth's poles. If the trend of rising temperatures continues, polar bears are likely to suffer. Polar bears prefer to travel and hunt for food on sea ice, but if the ice continues to melt, they won't be able to sustain themselves and numbers will reduce. There are currently between 20,000 and 28,000 polar bears, but the World Conservation Union estimates that numbers could drop by as much as a third by the year 2050.

Planet Watch

» Global warming is causing the famous snows and glaciers that top Tanzania's 3.7 mile (5,895 m) Mount Kilimanjaro to disappear. A third of the ice melted in the last two decades of the twentieth century.

» Studies show that wildlife behavior has changed to adapt to early springs in the Arctic. Wading birds have been laying eggs up to 10 days earlier than usual.

Flooding

The climate of a region is delicately balanced, and all kinds of factors can influence and change it. The future effects of climate change are difficult to predict precisely, but a clearer picture is emerging—the world is warming up, and this is already causing more unusual weather patterns. One of the most serious consequences of global warming is flooding.

As glaciers reduce and ice caps shrink, rising sea levels will have a direct environmental impact—up to half of the world's coastal wetlands will be covered in sea water by 2080. At the moment, glaciers and ice caps make up nearly one 10th of the Earth's land surface. As the ice melts, sea levels may rise by up to 3.3 feet (1 m) by the end of the century. Rising sea levels will flood the wetlands and other low-lying lands, erode beaches, and intensify flooding. The inflow of sea water will also turn rivers and underground aquifers salty, making the water unfit for use.

The effects of Hurricane Katrina, in August 2005, caused flooding in almost 80 percent of the city of New Orleans.

The islands of the Maldives are slowly going underwater as global warming causes sea levels to rise.

The Maldives

The Maldives is a group of more than 1,000 small islands located in the Indian Ocean, off the southern tip of India. Well known as an idyllic tourist location, the islands are becoming famous for another reason—their vulnerability. The highest point is just over 6.6 feet (2 m) above sea level. According to the Intergovernmental Panel on Climate Change (IPCC), a scientific body set up by the United Nations, sea levels could rise by up to 3.3 feet (1 m) by 2100. This would submerge 80 percent of the Maldives. Maumoon Abdul Gayoom, President of the Maldives, has pleaded with world leaders to reduce carbon dioxide emissions: "As a result of global warming and sea level rise, my country may disappear from the face of the Earth."

Drought

Drought is another extreme of climate change that can affect water distribution. In drought years, thousands of people may die in desert regions because of a lack of water and food. Heat waves are likely to become more intense and more frequent, and greater evaporation in the summer months means that droughts and wildfires will become more common. We could see millions of people around the world affected by food and water shortages in the coming years.

PLANET WATCH

» In 2006, floods affected 87 countries and were responsible for more deaths than any other weather-related disaster.

» In 2002, the 551 billion ton (500 billion t) Larsen B ice shelf in the Antarctic, an area the size of Rhode Island, disintegrated in less than a month.

» According to the British Antarctic Survey (BAS), more than 5,000 square miles (13,000 sq km) of sea ice in the Antarctic Peninsula have been lost over the last 50 years.

5 WATER IN THE FUTURE

All around the world, people's actions have caused a shortage of water. We continue to pollute water supplies, too. What hope is there for the future?

What Are Governments Doing?

In 2005, an international agreement on climate change came into force called the Kyoto Protocol. Negotiations for this international treaty began in 1997, when more than 150 countries met in Kyoto, Japan. They agreed to set targets to cut carbon emissions in an attempt to prevent the rise in global warming. In particular, MEDCs agreed to reduce their carbon emissions while helping LEDCs to develop as nations, but keep their carbon emissions low. World leaders, politicians, and scientists debated for more than seven years before countries committed to the treaty.

Earth Data

• In 2002, Israel accused Lebanon of taking water illegally from the Jordan River and threatened to go to war. The Hasbani River rises in Lebanon, before joining the Jordan River and the Sea of Galilee in Israel.

• A survey in 2003 by the Australian Food and Grocery Council showed that Australia was wasting about 2.4 million tons (2.2 million t) of food every year. The water used to produce this food could have supplied all the households in Sydney and Melbourne with enough water for a year.

In 2005, world leaders met in Kyoto, Japan, to commemorate the Kyoto Protocol. More than 180 countries have now agreed to cut carbon emissions.

Countries in central Asia have now agreed to cooperate to protect the Aral Sea. This inland sea shrunk to one-tenth of its size after rivers feeding it were diverted to irrigate cotton fields.

The countries that signed have now committed to reduce emissions by an average of about five percent of their 1990 levels by the period 2008–12. Some LEDCs, such as Brazil, India, and China, are not required to cut emissions, but simply to monitor them. At the moment, countries that are still developing do not feel that cutting carbon emissions is the fairest way for them to address the problem.

Flaws in the Treaty

The Kyoto Protocol has the support of nations that produce more than 60 percent of carbon dioxide emissions. However, the United States—the world's second biggest greenhouse gas polluter—has signed but not yet approved the treaty. The United States feels that reducing carbon emissions would have a serious effect on their economy. They claim they would only join if some LEDCs sign up, too. China, which produces more carbon emissions than any other country, is planning to join at the next round (after 2012)—as long as the United States has begun to cut emissions. Many of the nations who signed up are already falling behind with their targets.

Despite its flaws, the Kyoto Protocol is the most far-reaching global consensus on environmental issues. Participating nations have come a long way in beginning to tackle the huge problem of climate change. However, a global problem requires a global solution, and all nations, whether they are developed or developing, need to commit to reducing their greenhouse gas emissions. This will in turn affect the future of our water supplies. Leaders and environmental experts are aware that, while we need to provide for our present needs, we must take care not to damage resources for the future. Water is arguably the most important resource that we have available to us.

Fighting for Water

In 1995, Ismail Serageldin, vice president of the World Bank, said that many twentieth-century wars had been about oil. He predicted that wars of the twenty-first century would be about water. With the world population increasing by more than a million people each week, demands for water supplies will increase, particularly where resources are shared by more than one country.

Finite Water Supplies

The IPCC (see page 31) predicts that if climate change continues, millions of people will die. Millions more are also expected to become **environmental refugees** because of extreme weather conditions, such as the **desertification** of land and continued flooding. Since it is impossible to increase our **finite** water supply, it is clear that the world has to manage available water more efficiently.

Water Management Projects

Since the year 2000, the United Nations's World Water Assessment Programme (WWAP) has been monitoring supplies of freshwater and seeking to improve the management, supply, and quality of freshwater resources around the world. The WWAP looks at global issues but also helps individual countries to access local freshwater resources effectively.

In the Lake Titicaca basin in South America, for example, the glaciers that provide water for cities and towns in Peru and Bolivia are beginning to melt and disappear due to climate change (see page 28). In 2001, WWAP set up a water transfer project from the nearby Misicuni river basin. The first stage of the project finished in April 2005, which saw the provision of 132 gallons (500 L) of water per second for the Bolivian city of Cochabamba. When the final stage is completed, this quantity of water is expected to increase to 5,283 gallons (20,000 L) per second.

Can Charities Help?

Nongovernmental organizations (**NGOs**) or charities, such as WaterAid, work to enable the world's poorest people to gain access to safe water and sanitation. They also educate communities about water hygiene. WaterAid supports campaigns such as the United Nations World Water Day. The charity tries to increase public awareness about the reality behind the statistic that one in five people in the world have no access to safe drinking water.

Charities such as WaterAid help communities with different water management projects.

Desalination

Managing freshwater is one of the biggest challenges the world has to face. Many people view **desalination** as part of the solution to the problem of water management. Desalination is a process that removes excess salt and other minerals from seawater so that it is suitable to use for the irrigation of dry land or for drinking purposes. Desalination could have great potential for many regions that have access to the salty seawater of the oceans but little freshwater. There are, however, several drawbacks with desalination. The process creates huge quantities of excess salt and is very expensive, requiring lots of energy. But despite the drawbacks, the development of desalination plants continues. In 2008, a report by the International Desalination Association counted more than 13,000 desalination plants around the world, producing 1.6 billion cubic feet (45 million cu m) of water every day.

PLANET WATCH

» Desalination is used in more than 100 countries of the world. Middle Eastern countries produce about three-quarters of the world's desalinated water.

» According to statistics from the International Desalination Association, about two-thirds of the world's desalinated water output is used for drinking water and about one-third for industrial purposes.

Seawater is forced through a special membrane that removes salt and allows freshwater through.

Desalination plants filter seawater to provide a supply of freshwater. Salt and minerals are discharged back into the sea.

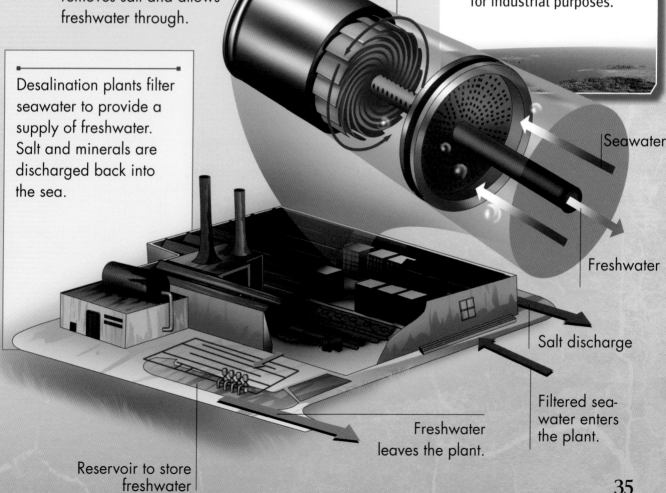

Seawater

Freshwater

Salt discharge

Filtered seawater enters the plant.

Freshwater leaves the plant.

Reservoir to store freshwater

Conventional methods of irrigation use a lot of water—much of it is wasted.

Irrigation

People have used irrigation to water the land for thousands of years. Irrigation techniques were used by the ancient civilizations of Egypt and Mesopotamia (present-day Iraq) as many as 8,000 years ago. Today there are many different irrigation techniques, but they all work on the same principle—that water is taken from a source, such as a river, lake, or aquifer, and distributed evenly across a field or region. Too much irrigation, however, can drain a water source dry. Irrigation methods can also waste a lot of water. According to the World Resources Institute (WRI), a U.S.-based environmental organization, 60 percent of irrigation water for crops never reaches its destination. "Drip irrigation" is a more efficient alternative. This method drips water on the roots of the plants to ensure minimum waste.

Water for Power

Another major use for the world's water, now and in the future, is in the generation of electricity. As fossil fuels decline, water is likely to play a big part in our energy needs. **Hydroelectric power** (HEP) currently supplies about 20 percent of the world's electricity. At a hydroelectric power station, a **dam** is built to form a reservoir. This provides water for farming and nearby homes. A gate controls the flow of water, which passes downhill from the dam through a channel. Here, it spins the blades of a water **turbine** connected to a generator that produces electricity. Hydroelectric power is a clean source of energy, creating less pollution than fossil fuels. However, when a dam is built, it can flood a whole valley. People may be forced to move their homes, and the natural habitats of plants and animals are destroyed.

The Rance River in France is home to a tidal power plant that harnesses the power of the tides to generate electricity.

Tidal Power

The energy of the seas and oceans could be a source of power for the future. Tides are caused by the moon's pull of gravity on the oceans. Tides rise and fall every day, giving a regular movement of seawater. In a tidal power plant, a gated barrier equipped with turbines is used to generate electricity when the tide flows in and out. Some parts of the world have stronger tides than others. Areas where the strong currents become concentrated—such as the entrance to a bay or a river, or the area between two land masses—are particularly suitable. Tidal power is a relatively new technology, but there are plans to develop a number of new sites around the world.

Wave Power

In the future, we are also likely to use the power of the ocean waves themselves. In 2006, Portugal built the world's first commercial wave farm, the Aguçadoura Wave Park near Póvoa de Varzim, to generate electricity. It uses a device called a Pelamis Wave Energy Converter. As the waves go past, the Pelamis bends up and down. This motion works pumps that turn a turbine to generate electricity. There are now plans to build wave power plants off the coast of Scotland and the coast of Cornwall in the United Kingdom.

PLANET WATCH

» According to a survey by UNESCO, in 2000, around 15 percent of the world's farming land was irrigated for food crops.

» Using water power, China's Three Gorges Dam on the Yangtze River will produce more electricity than any other dam in the world. When it is finished in 2011, it will supply one-tenth of China's electricity.

Saving Water

As freshwater becomes scarce in many regions, it has become clear that we need to work together to conserve water. On a global scale, the United Nations has identified two key areas to help save freshwater. The first is a cleanup campaign to clean all freshwater resources. The second covers water-saving projects around the world.

Technology can help us to conserve water in some areas. In farming, for example, soil moisture sensors stop irrigation systems when there is enough moisture in the soil. But we all need to be more water aware. Saving water in our offices and homes is one small step we can take immediately.

This woman is helping to clean up Muir Beach in California. Many volunteer organizations help to keep seawater safe from polluting garbage.

Doing Your Part

There are many small things that we can all do today to help cut down on water waste. Here are just a few examples:

- Turn off the tap when you brush your teeth.
- Take a short shower, not a bath.
- Turn taps off properly so they do not drip.
- Fix any leaks or drips immediately.
- Use a watering can, rather than a hose or sprinkler, to water the garden.
- Collect rainwater in a water barrel to water the garden.
- Use your washing machine and dishwasher only when they are full.
- Chill tap water in the fridge instead of buying bottled water.
- Never pour paint, oil, or bleach down the drain. Take them to a recycling center.
- Always avoid unnecessary waste. Reduce, reuse, and recycle.

Don't Waste It

When one in five people in the world do not have access to safe water, it is unfair that others waste water and needlessly pollute it. Some countries now use water meters to measure the quantity of water used by people and industries. Many people do not like this system, but it is one way of making us appreciate the value of water. It is time for us to change our attitude to water. We should never waste this precious resource—we need to act now before it is too late.

> In drought conditions, governments sometimes ban the use of hoses and sprinklers to help conserve water.

PLANET WATCH

» In 1992, the U.N. General Assembly declared that March 22 was "World Water Day." This day is now used to draw attention to the largest public health issue of our time—the global scarcity of clean water.

» Rainwater harvesting has become a popular way of saving water. Rainwater harvesting systems are used to collect rainwater from large areas, such as the roofs of buildings, to be stored for later use.

Facts and Figures

Hidden Uses of Water

Manufactured Goods

Just about everything we buy needs water to manufacture it. There are some surprises among these "hidden uses" of water.

Newspaper = 8 gallons (30 L)
Microchip = 8 gallons (30 L)
Aluminum can = 26 gallons (100 L)
Cloth diaper = 264 gallons (1,000 L)
Cotton T-shirt = 793 gallons (3,000 L)
Pair of leather shoes = 2,113 gallons (8,000 L)
Pair of jeans = 2,906 gallons (11,000 L)
Car = 105,669 gallons (400,000 L)

Food and Drink

Although the water needed to manufacture a car is an astonishing amount, it is not until we take into account food and drink that the true picture of water consumption emerges. Everything we eat and drink takes water to produce it—and we're talking enormous amounts of water! This hidden water is known as "embedded water." Although countries in northern Europe have plenty of rain, imported crops are more likely to have been irrigated using water pumped from aquifers or collected from rivers—they are more costly in the amount of water needed to produce them. Is it time for food manufacturers to state on the packaging how much water was used to produce or grow each product?

How Much Water Does It Take to Produce?

1 pound (.45 kg) potatoes = 60 gallons (225 L)
1 pound (.45 kg) wheat = 119 gallons (450 L)
1 pound (.45 kg) sugar = 238 gallons (900 L)
1 pound (.45 kg) rice = 357 gallons (1,350 L)
1 pound (.45 kg) eggs = 357 gallons (1,350 L)
1 pound (.45 kg) chicken = 476 gallons (1,800 L)
1 pound (.45 kg) cheese = 595 gallons (2,250 L)
1 pound (.45 kg) cotton = 951 gallons (3,600 L)
1 pound (.45 kg) black tea = 1,070 gallons (4,050 L)
1 pound (.45 kg) coffee = 2,378 gallons (9,000 L)

The Global Water Footprint

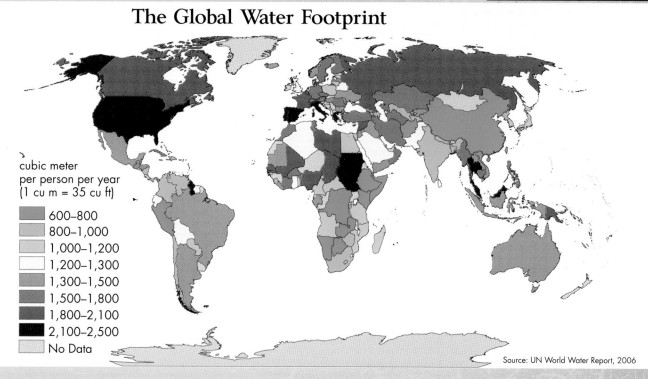

cubic meter
per person per year
(1 cu m = 35 cu ft)

- 600–800
- 800–1,000
- 1,000–1,200
- 1,200–1,300
- 1,300–1,500
- 1,500–1,800
- 1,800–2,100
- 2,100–2,500
- No Data

Source: UN World Water Report, 2006

The water footprint of a country refers to the sum of direct and indirect fresh-water use by the consumer. The direct water use is the water used by homes and industries. The indirect water use relates to the total volume of freshwater that is used to produce the goods and services consumed by the nation.

How Much Water Does Each Person Use per Day?

Australia = 130 gal (493 L)
Cambodia = 4 gal (15 L)
China = 23 gal (86 L)
India = 36 gal (135 L)
Japan = 99 gal (374 L)
Mozambique = 1 gal (4 L)
Nigeria = 10 gal (36 L)
Spain = 85 gal (320 L)
UK = 40 gal (150 L)
USA = 152 gal (575 L)

The above figures show the average amount of water used in each country for activities such as drinking, washing, cooking, and cleaning. But when we factor in the "embedded water" used, particularly hidden in food and drink, the average person in the United States uses much more than 152 gallons (575 L) of water per day. It exceeds 1,321 gallons (5,000 L)!

Glossary

alkaline
describing a soluble substance that can neutralize an acid

aquatic
found in water

aquifer
an underground rock, such as sandstone, containing water

atom
a basic building block of matter

carbon emissions
gases containing carbon, released when a fuel is burned, for example

central nervous system
nerve tissue of the brain and spinal cord

climate
the average weather of a region over a period of many years

contaminate
to pollute by something impure

cyclone
a violent tropical storm

dam
a barrier to stop the flow of water

decompose
to decay or break down

delta
flat land at the mouth of a river, where the main stream splits into several branches

desalination
the process of removing salt, especially from seawater

desertification
the process of fertile land turning into desert

detergent
a cleansing agent, widely used in the home

diarrhea
a condition where the body loses water in the feces

dissolve
to make into a liquid

drought
a long period with little rainfall

ecological
to do with ecology, the study of relationships between living organisms and their environment

ecosystem
all the living things in an environment and the way in which they work together

environmental refugees
people forced to leave their region or country due to environmental factors, such as desertification

evaporation
to change from a liquid (or solid) state to a gas, or vapor

fertilizer
a substance (usually chemical) added to soil or water to increase the amount of crops it can produce

food chain
a group of animals in which each member is in turn eaten by another in the chain

food web
a complex of interrelated food chains

finite
limited or restricted in nature

friendly bacteria
bacteria that are not harmful

glacier
a slow-moving mass of ice

global warming
the gradual warming of the Earth's climate

greenhouse gases
gases in the atmosphere that absorb heat from the sun and prevent it from escaping into space

Gulf Stream
the warm ocean current of the northern Atlantic Ocean off eastern North America

hydroelectric power
electricity made from water power

ice floe
a sheet of ice floating in the sea

irrigation
a method of supplying farmland with water, often using channels and ditches

latitude
a region of the Earth measured in relation to its distance from the equator

LEDCs
short for less economically developed countries, or the poorer countries of the world

MEDCs
short for more economically developed countries, or the richer countries of the world

microbes
tiny living things too small to see without a microscope

molecule
a particle made from two or more atoms joined together

neutralize
to make chemically neutral

NGO
a nongovernmental organization, which is often a charity

pH value
a measurement of how acidic or alkaline a solution is. 7 is neutral on the scale, 0 is very acidic, and 14 is very alkaline.

photosynthesis
the process by which green plants use sunlight to create energy in the form of carbohydrates

pollution
the effect of poisonous or harmful substances that are released into the environment

porous
able to absorb water, for example, like a sponge

precipitation
rain, sleet, snow, or hail formed by condensation of water vapor

purification
the act of cleansing or purifying

reservoir
a lake used for storing water, often behind a dam

sanitation
the use of measures to protect and maintain public health, including drainage and disposal of sewage

slick
a floating film of oil

sludge
the solids in sewage

solvent
a liquid that is able to dissolve a solid

tide
the alternate rise and fall of sea level

toxic
poisonous

turbine
an engine powered by blades that extract energy from a flow of fluids

ultraviolet (UV) light
radiation lying in the ultraviolet range; wavelengths that are shorter than light, but longer than X-rays

FURTHER READING

- *Drought* (Wild Weather) by Catherine Chambers (Heinemann, 2007)
- *Protecting Earth's Water Supply* (Saving Our Living Earth) by Ron Fridell (Lerner Publications, 2009)
- *Water* (Managing Our Resources) by Ian Graham (Heinemann, 2005)
- *Water* (See for Yourself) by Trevor Day (DK Publishing, 2007)
- *Water Power* (Energy Sources) by Neil Morris (Smart Apple Media, 2007)

INDEX

WEB FINDER

http://ga.water.usgs.gov/edu/
This web site is packed with information about water on Earth and how we use it.

www.dcwasa.com/kids
This web site includes a water calculator for estimating water use per household.

www.waterfootprint.org
Facts about your water footprint and how you can reduce it.

www.epa.gov/OGWDW/kids
Lots of information on water from the Environmental Protection Agency.

www.water.org/waterpartners.aspx?pgID=916
Facts about water, drinking water, and water-related diseases.

www.wateraid.org/splash_out/facts/4872.asp
Amazing facts about water and links to some water games.